The Party Book

Jane Bull

Dorling Kindersley

LONDON, NEW YORK, MUNICH,
MELBOURNE, AND DELHI

DESIGN • Jane Bull
TEXT • Penelope Arlon
PHOTOGRAPHY • Andy Crawford
DESIGN ASSISTANCE • Sadie Thomas

PUBLISHING MANAGER • Sue Leonard
MANAGING ART EDITOR • Clare Shedden
PRODUCTION • Shivani Pandey
DTP DESIGNER • Almudena Díaz
JACKET DESIGNER • Chris Drew

For Charlotte, Billy, and James
First published in Great Britain in 2005 by
Dorling Kindersley Limited
80 Strand, London WC2R 0RL

A Penguin Company

2 4 6 8 10 9 7 5 3

A CIP catalogue record for this book
is available from the British Library

ISBN: 1-4053-0842-7

Colour reproduction by
GRB Editrice S.r.l., Verona, Italy
Printed and bound in China by Toppan

discover more at
www.dk.com

Let's party

A book full of parties . . .

What kind of party?

Here are some ideas that you can follow in the book.

Party theme

The first decision to make is what theme to have. Are you planning a birthday treat, such as a trip to a zoo or a racetrack? This might be your chosen theme.

Spooky!

It's hot outside – let's create a water theme and swim with the **fishes**...

Party craft

Get your guests to make something that ties in with the party theme, and they can take their project home.

We're going to the zoo so why not try some **Jungle fun?**

Games

Most of the games in this book, such as the fishing game or treasure hunt, can be adapted to any theme, so use your imagination.

Invitation to a party!

to: Guest's name

please come to my party

on: Date – include the day of the week

at: Address where the party will take place

time: When the party begins... and ends

r.s.v.p. This asks guests to reply so you will know whether or not they can come. Give them an address or phone number they can reply to.

ALSO you may want to remind guests to dress up/bring a mask/wear swimming costumes etc.

Party tips

o **How long?** About two and a half hours is about right. This will give you time to greet your guests, get crafty, play games, eat the birthday tea, say goodbye and hand out party bags.

o **How many?** Five or seven guests work well. (When you join in, there will be an even number.)

o **Be prepared** Keep things simple and make sure everything is organized before the party starts.

o **Start the fun** When guests arrive, show them to the craft table. This will help everyone to relax and settle in.

o **Don't** give out your invitations at school – unless you want the whole class to come.

o **Do** have prizes for everyone, not just guests who win games.

Have fun with your friends!

Wings and Wishes

Only fairies and princesses with wings and wands are welcome to flutter by this party and make wishes come true.

To Lucy

Wear your best fairy wings

Come to my
Wings and Wishes
PARTY
on 4th April
at my house
3.00pm to 6.00pm

Love Tara

r.s.v.p.

Lucy

6

7

Fairy food

Sparkly stars, wands, and butterfly biscuits help to feed the fairies at your party. Little cakes, each with a candle, mean all your guests can make a wish of their own.

Table top

Try this idea for your table centrepiece. Raise your cakes by sitting them on a decorated container, and position your tasty treats into fairy rings around it.

Wishing wands

Party bag bundle

Paper cup

Fairy cakes

Glue paper hearts to the edge of a cake board.

Stick hearts on paper cups.

Bake a biscuit on a lolly stick.

Cut two slices of bread into heart shapes and remove a smaller heart from one of them (page 44). Spread jam on the solid slice, then squash the two together.

Make-a-wish cakes

Jammy hearts

Sweet wings

Flying biscuits

Butterfly biscuits

Sweet hearts

Recipes

Find out how to make these sweet cakes and biscuits by turning to pages 44-48.

Party activity table

Get your fairy guests to create beautiful butterflies, and hang them up during the party. When it's time to go home, they can fly away with them.

PAPER PLATES

Cut out lots of pink paper hearts.

FELT PENS

GLUE STICK

SCISSORS

Stick heart shapes on the plates to make a string of fluttering butterflies.

Heart invitation

Make extra-special, home-made heart invitations and send them to your best friends.

How to make a heart shape

Take a piece of tracing paper and fold it in half. With the fold down the edge of the page, trace around this half heart shape. Cut it out; when you open it, you should have a perfect heart template to draw around (turn to page 36).

You can also use this template for the heart shapes on the banners.

Choose colourful pieces of paper, or decorate them yourself.

Draw around your heart template (see page 36).

Cut out as many as you need.

Write your party invitation before you fold it up.

Fold the two sides into the centre.

Fold the top of the heart down.

Fold the bottom of the heart up.

Use a sticker to seal the flap.

Write your guest's name on the sticker.

Fairy fun and games

Start

Party prizes

These dainty fairy bundles are made out of light fabric like netting or tissue paper.

Cut out two pieces of fabric or tissue and layer one on top of the other.

Pile sweets or toys in the middle.

Elastic band

Gather up the fabric and tie it in a bundle with an elastic band.

Finish off the bags with extra toys or a pretty ribbon.

Fairy trails

Send your fairy friends fluttering out into the garden to follow your trails. Use confetti or sweets laid in arrow shapes to point them towards the treasure.
At the end there are treats for ALL.

Wishing well

Fish for wishes with a magic wand. Catch a star on the end of your line and find out if you win a prize or have to do a forfeit.

Tie a magnet to the end of the wand with a piece of string.

Write a forfeit or a prize on each heart.

Put a paper clip onto each heart.

The magnet will pick up the paper-clip hearts.

Finish
Collect a prize

Fins and Fishes

Set sail for watery party fun. Can you find the hidden treasure in the old pirate wreck?

To
William

Come to
a Water Party

Bring your swimmers!

Setting sail on Saturday 6th June at 3.00pm.
Meet up at Jimmy's house.

Don't forget your flippers

Fishy food
Serve up biscuits
and snacks from big
paper boats, all washed
down with waves of
ocean punch.

Table top
Use a big bright towel as
a tablecloth, your (clean)
beach buckets as containers,
and a large fishbowl to serve
up your punch.

Ocean punch
Icy lemonade with a
few drops of blue
food colouring.

Recipes
See pages 42-48 for
how to make drinks,
cookies, and cupcakes.

Snack boats
Make big paper boats – turn
to page 16 to find out how
– and fill them with all sorts
of snacks.

14

Party activity table

Get your guests to create their own fantasy jellyfish. Then hang them up while the party's on, and when it's home time they can swim off with them.

PAPER BOWL

STRING

STICKY TAPE

GLUE STICK

SCISSORS

TISSUE PAPER

Pierce the bottom of the bowl and thread the string through.

Tape the string in place.

Stick strips of paper to the bottom of your bowl.

Let's hang around at the party!

Cut out eyes and spots to glue on.

Island cupcakes

Brown sugar looks like a sandy beach.

Pick-a pot

Empty ice-cream cones

Fill with biscuits, sweets, and fruit.

Don't forget the ice lollies!

Boat invitation

Send a boat out to each of your guests with the details of your party on the outside. Make a small boat for the invitation and use larger paper to make big boats for your food table.

PAPER

20 x 30 CM
(8 x 11 IN)

Fold the piece of paper in half.

Fold in half again to find the middle, then open out.

Fold one corner into the centre.

Fold the other corner to the middle.

Turn up the bottom flap as far as it will go.

Turn it over and fold up the flap on this side.

Pull the boat open and fold down the other way.

Starfish shape
Use this template to make your starfish banner. To learn how to do this, turn to page 36.

Turn over and fold up the flap on this side.

Tuck the loose edges under.

Turn up the bottom flap.

Pull the bottom open and fold down the other way.

Pull the corners apart and open out.

Open up and fold the shape flat.

Bigger bits of paper make bigger boats

Pull open the bottom of the boat to make it stand up.

16

Watery fun and games

Party prizes

Paper cups make perfect little beach buckets to pack with party treats.

PAPER CUP

Make a small hole each side of the cup.

Cut a thin paper strip.

PAPER STRIP HANDLE

PAPER FASTENERS

2 x 16 cm (3/4 x 6 in)

Attach the handle to the cup using the paper fasteners.

Fill up your buckets with goodies

William

Water bombs

Who can splash the most balloons in the the target? Use a paddling pool and a rubber ring as a target. Fill up lots of balloons with water in advance. Let each person take turns to try and hit the ring target.

Can you hit the target?

Yes! Top score

Water balloons

Go fishing

Cut out all sorts of sea creatures and attach paper clips to each. Make a fishing rod from a stick and string, and tie a magnet on the end. Who can catch the creature with the shiny fin? Every catch wins a treat, but only the creature with the glittery scale will win a bonus prize.

STRING AND STICK

MAGNET

PAPER CLIP

PAPER FISH

Ghouls and Ghosts

Enter if you dare – get into the spirit of this spooky party and prepare for the groaning feast.

Come to a
Ghouls
and
Ghosts
party

Who goes there!

Ghoulish feast

Fill a bowl with popcorn, throw in a few jelly snakes, and add eyes and a drooling mouth. Food on sticks makes scary-looking snacks – try marshmallow eyeballs with black gumdrop pupils.

Table top

Cover your table with black plastic bin-liners, and add strips of red paper that look like bloody drips.

Stick the gruesome eyeballs on sticks.

Bowl of popcorn

Jelly snakes and liquorice sticks

Cut out ghoulish details and stick them to the bowl.

Make a blood-thirsty drink by adding red food colouring to lemonade.

Stick cut-out spider shapes on red paper cups.

Spiders and giant's eyes stare you in the face

20

Creepy cupcakes

Find out how to make and decorate cupcakes and biscuits on page 44

Spooks on sticks

Ghost-shaped
biscuits on a stick
(see page 48).

Party pokers

Red and
black sweets
on a stick

Wooden
skewers

Cherry tomatoes,
baby sausages,
red peppers, and
cheese on sticks

Tape the straight end to a doorway
for an upside-down spook!

Let us hang around at your party

Party activity table

Get your guests to help with the decorations
by making paper ghosts. Hang these up while
the party is on and when it's home time they
can fly away.

ROLL OF GREASEPROOF PAPER

Cut off
the top in
a straight
line.

Roll out a length of greaseproof
paper and draw on your spook.
Then cut it out.

A ghostly invitation

This pop-up card will certainly put the shivers into any guests. Will they be brave enough to turn up?

Ghost shape

Use this template to cut out ghost shapes for your banners. Turn to page 36 for full instructions.

1 Take a piece of black card and fold it in half with the fold on the left.

Cut two slits 2 cm (1 in) across that are 2 cm (1 in) apart and up from the bottom.

Fold over the resulting paper flap and press hard on the crease to make it sharp.

Open up the card and push the slit square out through the front.

2

Cut out a spook.

Stick the bottom of the spook to the front of the slit flap.

GLUE STICK

Draw me a face in black pen.

Write your invitation on a red blobby shape.

When the card opens, the spook will jump out!

3 Close the card and decorate the front.

To make a blob, fold over a piece of paper and draw half your design.

Cut it out and unfold it.

Glue it to the outside of the card to hide the gap.

Smooth it down.

Don't glue over this bit.

22

Party prizes

Hand out these spooky bundles, made with paper or white material, as prizes or goody bags.

CREPE PAPER

TOYS AND SWEETS

Place toys or sweets in the centre.

Bind up with elastic bands.

Glue on spooky black paper faces.

Begin here

House of horrors

Send your guests off to look for hidden treats following your spooky treasure-hunt trail. Leave creepy signs around your house that will send them to the next clue. If possible, set up scary lights and ghoulish ghosts to give them a fright or two as they make their way.

Candles make spooky lights.

Is it up the stairs?

Try some of my drink – I dare you.

Keep going, not long now

Creepy Parcel

Before the party wrap a prize in layers of paper – use newspaper, black crepe or tissue paper, or even toilet paper to make it look like a mummy. Tuck a small treat inside each one. When you're ready, sit everyone in a circle, choose some spooky music, and get an adult to turn it on and off. When the music starts, pass the parcel around. When the music stops, the person holding it unwraps the top layer and keeps the treat. Keep going until one lucky person reaches the prize in the middle.

Now delve in to find a treat

The end

Guess whoooooo…

Jungle Fun

Deep in the jungle – come and monkey about with the other wild creatures at the party.

To Simon

Please come to my
Jungle Fun party
◆ on the ◆
8th October
4.00 – 6.00pm.

r.s.v.p.

Get ready for a wild time!

Jungle juice

It's feeding time in the tropics –
serve up cupcake creatures and tangy fruits and slurp refreshing jungle juice.

Table top

Keep it green! Lots of different shades (like a leaf-coloured cloth) will make your room look like a jungle. Any toy animals you have will fit the theme perfectly.

Decorate paper cups with flowers made from card.

Watering hole

Stir bits of fruit into green jelly to make a yummy jungle pond.

Make jungle juice by adding green food colouring to lemonade.

Cupcake creatures

Recipes

Find out how to make these cakes and biscuits on pages 44-48.

Veggie sticks

Pieces of raw vegetable on skewers can look like exotic foliage.

Nectar pools

Sweets in jelly look like delicious nectar pools.

Fruity flower

Cut out half a melon in a zig-zag shape and fill it with grapes and strawberries.

Party activity table

Ask your guests to create swirling snakes. Hang these all around while the party's on, and when it's home time they can slither away.

Place a paper plate on a piece of green paper and draw around it.

Starting from the edge, draw a non-stop swirl all the way to the centre.

Now cut your swirl from the outside to the middle. Round off the end to make the head.

Decorate the body using stickers or pieces of coloured card.

Tape a piece of string to the centre of the tail and let your snake dangle.

Mask
invitation

Send these mask invitations out to each guest so they can all arrive at your party ready for jungle fun.

PAPER PLATE

PARTY HOOTER

ELASTIC

COLOURED PAPER FACES

Cut out a green shape the width of the plate but slightly less high.

SCISSORS

GLUE STICK

Use this template to make a treetop banner. To find out how, turn to page 36.

1 Attach the paper shapes onto the plate using glue stick.

Cut a dark-green strip to make a wide mouth, then two red spots for eyes.

2 Make two nose holes with a ballpoint pen.

The nose holes are for you to see through, so make sure they sit exactly where your eyes will go.

3 Make two more holes at the edges for the elastic.

Thread elastic through them and knot the ends to hold it in place.

4

Ribbit ribbit!

Finally make a big hole for the mouth and stick the squeaker through it.

Jungle fun and games

Monkey statues

This is an active game. Ask a grown-up to put some music on, then – from time to time – turn it off again. Your guests should all dance like monkeys until the music stops, when they must keep very still. Anyone caught twitching is sent out of the jungle. The final survivor is the winner.

Ribbit ribbit

Party prizes

Make snake goody bags by packing new green knee socks with treats. Complete each pair by tucking the other sock inside as well.

Cut out shapes from felt and glue them on the stuffed sock.

Close the top with an elastic band.

Hisssss! prizzzzzessss

Painting jungle faces

Create exotic and fearsome beasts with face paint – on your hands!

SPONGE

FACE PAINTS

You will need:
FACE PAINTS
WATER
PAINT BRUSHES
SPONGES

Use a brush to paint the teeth.

Cover the hand in one colour.

Mix the paint colours to create different shades.

• Wet the sponge and dip it in the paint.
• Paint your hand with the main colour.
• Add the details with a brush.

Wacky Wheels

From racing cars to trucks, get ready for a fast party of wheelies and spins.

To Thomas, come to a Wacky Wheels party

Spin the wheel for details

Satur

bring a c

Bring along your favourite vehicle

Party pit-stop

Wheel in the goodies – plan your party using bright warning colours like yellow, orange, and red with black.

Table top

Build up your party table by placing a decorated plate or tray on a round cake tin and displaying your food around a traffic cone. Search your room for any toy cars or trucks, and anything else with wheels that will add to the theme.

Make your own winner's flags for the top of your display.

Use a toy plastic traffic cone.

Tool-box goodies

Decorate goodie bags and boxes to look like a tool kits.

Try to find cakes that already have round swirls or are chequered.

Cut a strip of yellow card to fit around the rim, stick black stripes across it and wrap the strip around the plate's edge.

Wicked wheel sandwiches

Recipes

Find out how to make the flag sandwich and sweet wheel by turning to page 43.

Find out how to make the flag sandwich and sweet wheel by turning to page 43.

Winner's flag sandwich

Mini sandwiches make up the giant flag – it can be as big as you like.

Sweet wheels

Make pictures from sweets and display them on plates.

Muffin transporter

Use your toys to serve up party treats.

Party activity table

Everyone's a winner with a chequered flag. Get your guests to add to the decorations during the party, then send them home with their own flag.

SCISSORS

GLUE

STRAW

BLACK AND WHITE PAPER

Cut a piece of white paper 8 x 12 cm (3¼ x 4¼ in).

Glue a straw to the edge.

Cut 20 black squares 2 x 2 cm (¾ x ¾ in).

Glue squares onto both sides of the white paper.

Now wave your flag

Wheelie invitation

1 Fold a piece of tracing paper in half. Lay it over the template with the folded edge on the left, and draw around the wheel.

2 Cut out the shape.

3 Trace around the shape onto a square of black paper, marking the centre point.

4 Cut out the wheel and make a small hole in the centre.

5 Cut the hubcap circle out of white or silver paper, then snip out one of these four shapes so the black card will show through.

6 Glue on three pieces of black paper to make the other three shapes.

Use a silver pen to write your invitation.

7 Fix the wheel and the hubcap together with a paper fastener.

To Thomas - Please come

Sat

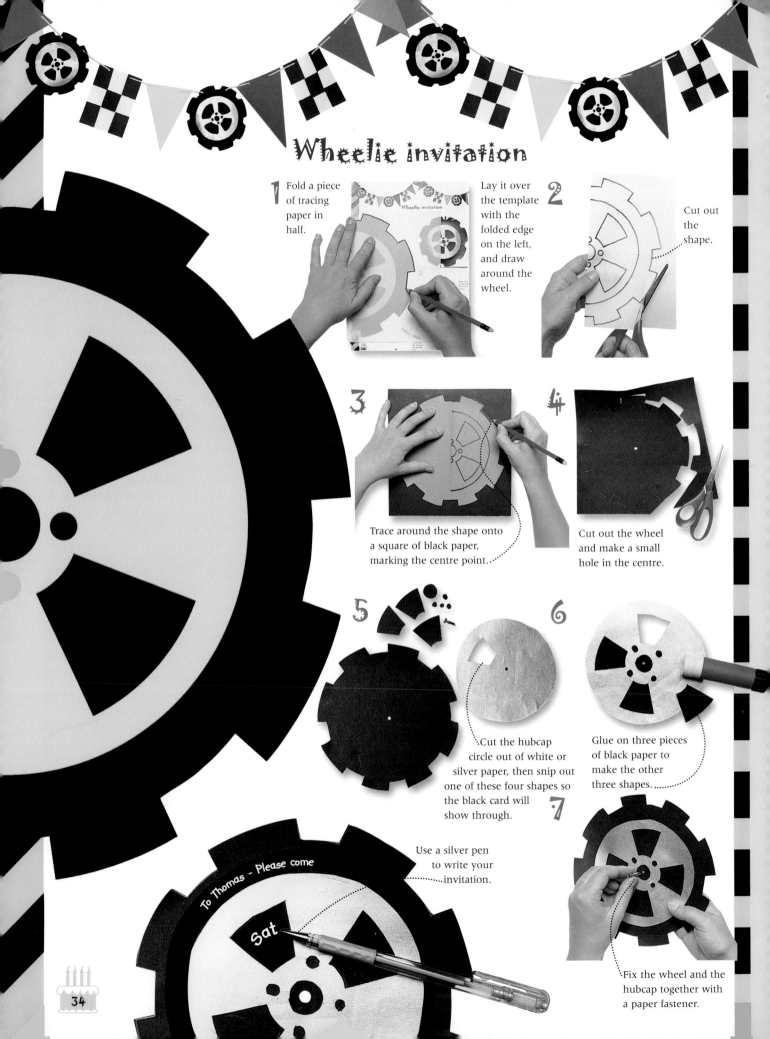

Wheelie fun and games

Party prizes

Use two paper plates decorated with the wheel shape to make a 3-D goody pack stuffed with wheely good stuff.

Fill a paper plate with goodies, then place another one on top.

Staple the two plates together all the way round.

Cut out two wheel shapes and stick one to each side of the goody pack.

Give away these wacky wheels

Treasure trip

Set a trail around your house or garden using home-made road signs to point your guests in the right direction.

Hide a prize at the end of the trail.

Use these 'no entry' signs to stop your drivers from going the wrong way.

Use these arrow signs to show your drivers where to go.

START

You are the winner!

Domino raceway

Make a fantastic raceway for your toy cars and see who can get to the finish line first. Start by turning empty kitchen and toilet rolls into tunnels. For ramps, cut them in half lengthwise. Small tables and stools make sturdy bridges.

Build a domino run by setting up the dominos carefully so a car will roll off the track and onto the first one.

After that, each domino should hit the one in front to keep the run going.

Paper-plate shapes

Lay a piece of tracing paper with the right half over the template and draw around the dotted line.

Templates

Throughout the party pages you will find templates. Use them to make hanging decorations or turn to page 38 to learn how to transform them into party banners.

Fold the tracing paper in half along the centre line.

Cut around the line.

Hold down the shape carefully.

Cut around the outline.

Draw around it on a piece of paper.

Punch holes in the top for the string.

Use glue stick to attach your shapes to paper plates.

Decorate your shape with paper, stickers, and coloured pens.

Fancy flowers

Screaming ghouls

Smiling sea creatures

Party banners

These decorations are simple and quick to put together using two or three basic shapes that suit your theme.

All you need are string, straws, and your paper shapes

Cut a piece of string the length you want your banner to be, and tie a knot at one end.

Thread the string through the straw...

...then through the first paper shape.

Attach more and more shapes until your banner is finished.

Hang 'em high

Whether you hang them against a wall or across
a room, these banners will look party fantastic.
Make them suit to whatever theme you choose.
If it's a special birthday, try spelling
out a message.

Large, small, and rainbow-coloured stars

Hanging stars

These instant decorations are very simple to make and create stunning effects – with rounded edges, for example, they look like flowers. Use coloured paper, or paint patterns on white paper.

PAPER
22 x 29 CM
(8 x 11 IN)

OR for larger or smaller stars, try whole sheets of wrapping paper or pages from magazines.

Fold the paper backwards and forwards in a concertina shape.

Fold the paper in the middle.

Cut across one corner.

Tape these two edges together.

Tape the other two edges together.

Attach a piece of string or ribbon for hanging.

Try all sorts of different paper to match your party theme.

Cool drinks

Colourful ice

1. Fill a jug with water.
2. Add a few drops of food colouring.
3. Mix it well.
4. Pour into an ice tray.
5. Place in the freezer overnight.

WATER   FOOD COLOURING

RUBBER GLOVE

BALLOON

Ice shapes

Use different containers such as jelly moulds or plastic bottle bases to make giant ice cubes. Or try soft moulds like rubber gloves or balloons – you'll have to tie them closed so the water won't leak out, then cut or tear them away when the ice has frozen.

PLASTIC BOTTLE BASES

JELLY MOULD

Watch your drinks change colour!

Party cups

Plain plastic or paper cups are easy to decorate. Either cut out shapes or strips from card and glue them on, or use stickers.

Swish sandwiches

Wicked wheels

Take a thin slice of light-coloured bread and cut off the crusts.

Spread it with a dark filling of your choice.

Roll the slice up tightly.

Use a sharp knife to cut it into pinwheels.

Winners flag

Take two slices of bread – one light coloured and one dark. Cut the crusts off both slices.

Spread one slice with a filling of your choice.

Place the other slice on top to make a sandwich.

Cut the sandwich into six rectangles.

Lay out the winning flag by turning over every other shape to make a chequerboard pattern.

For a bigger flag, add more shapes.

Cookies

Makes 24
small biscuits

Plain
flour
300 g (6 oz)

Butter
200 g (4 oz)

Castor
sugar
100 g (2 oz)

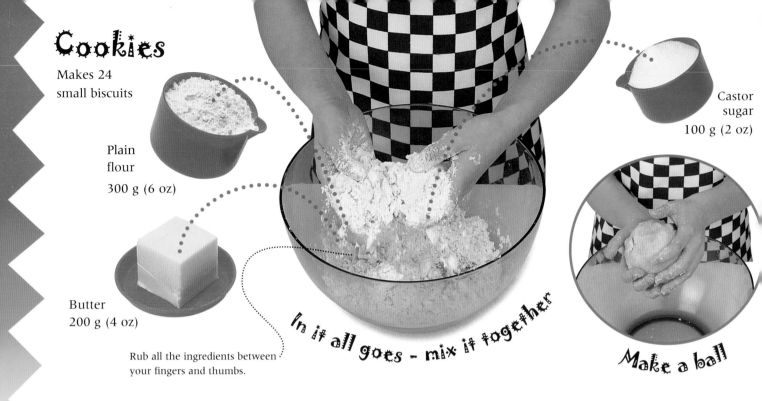

Rub all the ingredients between
your fingers and thumbs.

In it all goes – mix it together

Make a ball

Making cookies and cupcakes

Cookies and cupcakes make the best party food, especially for themed parties because you can decorate them any way you like and they always taste delicious.

Cupcakes

Makes 16
cupcakes

Castor
sugar
125 g (4 oz)

Butter
125 g (4 oz)

2 eggs

Self-raising flour
125 g (4 oz)

Vanilla essence
few drops

Put everything in a bowl and whisk it

Baking powder
1 tsp

44

Set the oven to
190°C, 375°F, Gas mark 5

1 Roll out the ball

Your dough should
be about .5 cm (¹/₄ in) thick.

Use cookie cutters
to cut out shapes.

2 Cut out the shapes

Place the
cookies on a
baking tray.

Bake them
for 15
minutes.

3 Bake the cookies

Ask an adult
to help with
the oven.

Smooth surface

When your shapes stick to the rolling
pin or the surface, they're more likely
to be damaged, so sprinkle everything
with flour before you begin.

Set the oven to
190°C, 375°F, Gas mark 5

Put a teaspoon
of mixture in
each case.

1 Fill up the paper cases

Bake the cupcakes
for 20 minutes.

2 In the oven

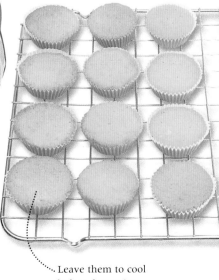

Leave them to cool
before decorating.

3 Let them cool

Decorate your fabulous feast

Now for the fun part. When your cookies and cakes are cool, it's time to decorate them. Turn back to the party pages to see how you would like them to look, then follow these hints and tips.

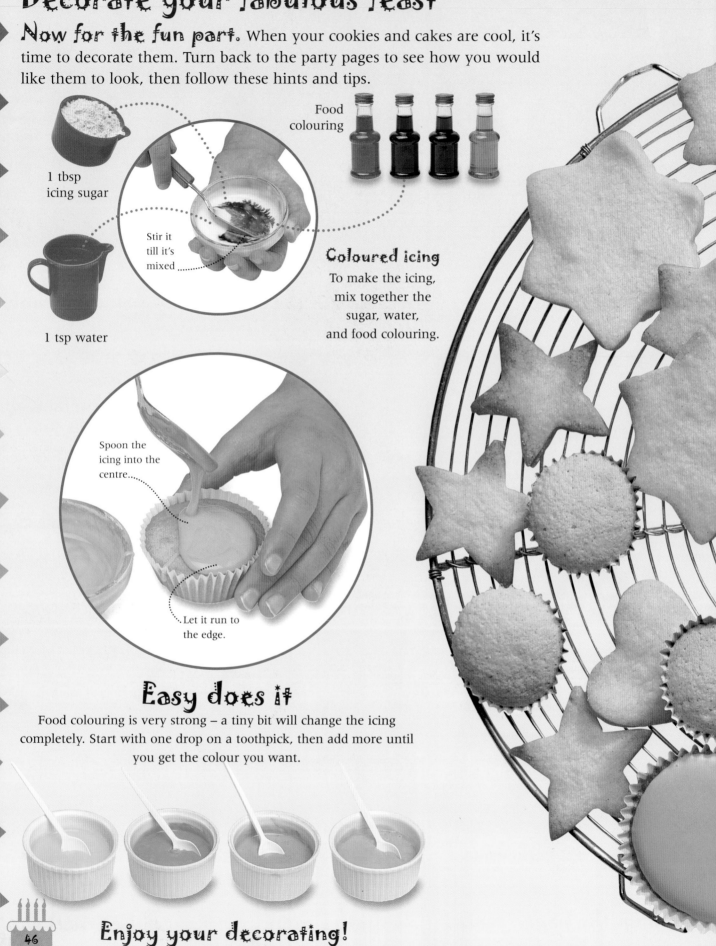

1 tbsp icing sugar

1 tsp water

Food colouring

Stir it till it's mixed

Coloured icing

To make the icing, mix together the sugar, water, and food colouring.

Spoon the icing into the centre...

...Let it run to the edge.

Easy does it

Food colouring is very strong – a tiny bit will change the icing completely. Start with one drop on a toothpick, then add more until you get the colour you want.

Enjoy your decorating!

Sweet decoration

Sweets are very useful for extra decoration.

Jelly sweets

Sugar strands

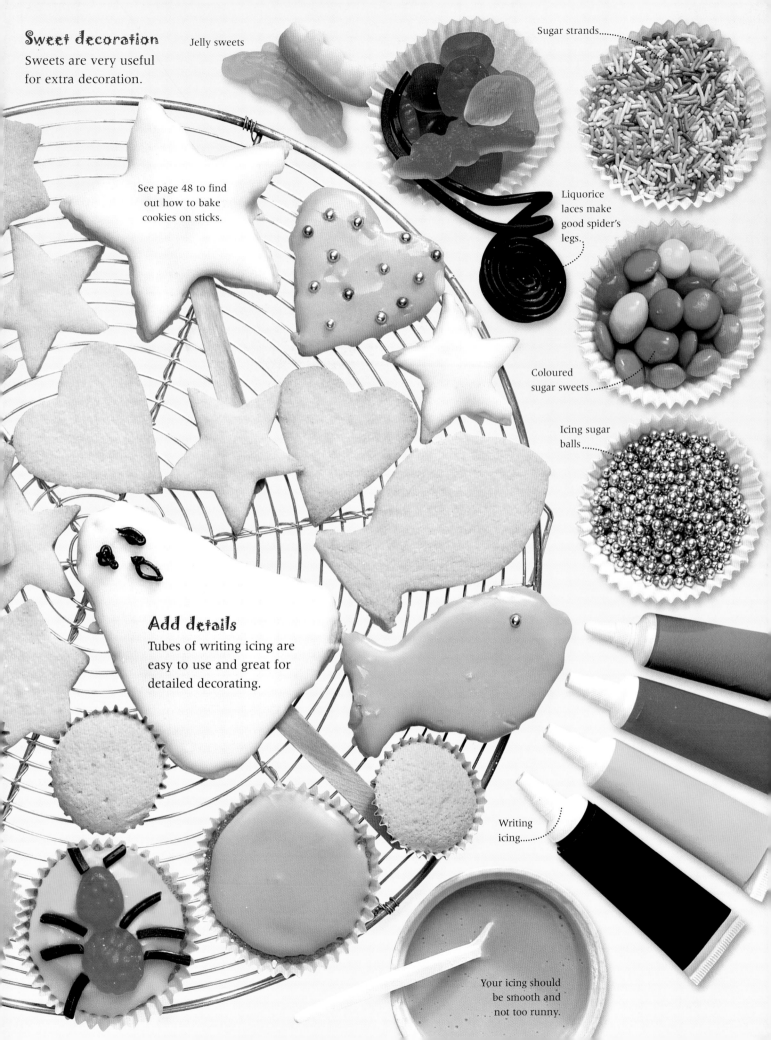

Liquorice laces make good spider's legs.

Coloured sugar sweets

Icing sugar balls

See page 48 to find out how to bake cookies on sticks.

Add details

Tubes of writing icing are easy to use and great for detailed decorating.

Writing icing

Your icing should be smooth and not too runny.

Suitable shapes

Draw your chosen shapes onto thin card and cut them out.

Place your cutouts onto rolled-out dough.

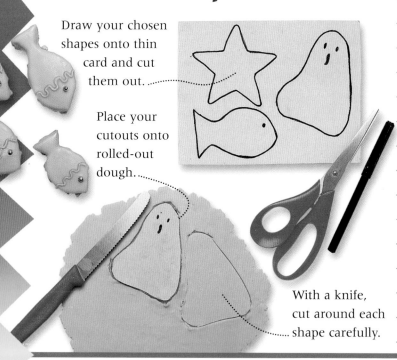

With a knife, cut around each shape carefully.

Baked lollies

Cut out two matching shapes.

Press the shapes together around the edges.

Press a lolly stick into one of them.

Place the other one on top.

TIP: Assemble your lollies on the baking tray so you don't have to move them.

Set the oven to 190C, 375F, Gas mark 5, and bake them for 20-25 minutes.

When they're cool, get decorating! (see page 46)

Acknowledgements

The publisher would like to thank Corbis/Laura Doss for permission to reproduce the image on the bottom of page 3. All other images © Dorling Kindersley.

For further information see: www.dkimages.com